COVID19 SUTRAS

Sutras 1-5

March 1, 2020 – June 13, 2020

Hank Lazer

Lavender Ink
New Orleans

COVID19 SUTRAS

Hank Lazer

Copyright © 2020 by Hank Lazer and Lavender Ink,
an imprint of Diálogos Books

Printed in the U.S.A.
First Printing
10 9 8 7 6 5 4 3 2 1   20 21 22 23 24 25

Cover photo by the author
Book design: Bill Lavender

Library of Congress Control Number: 2020941847
Lazer, Hank
COVID19 SUTRAS / Hank Lazer
p. cm.

ISBN: 978-1-944884-86-4   (pbk.)

Lavender Ink
lavenderink.org

Acknowledgement:
Chant de la Sirène, The Journal (Issue 1—online)—sections
from Sutra #4 – thanks to editor Laura Hinton

To Joseph Lease
To Lynn Snow

    & to the Quiet Tide Sangha
    & the Tuscaloosa Zen Meditation Circle

You have gained the pivotal opportunity of human form. Do not use your time in vain. You are maintaining the essential working of the buddha way. Who would take wasteful delight in the spark from the flintstone? Besides, form and substance are like the dew on the grass, destiny like the dart of lightning—emptied in an instant, vanished in a flash.

—Dogen, *Fukanzazengi*

COVID19 SUTRA 1

(early days)

books & blossoms
spring & all
cold morning no
wind cloud bank

over the mountain
ridge city & its
tower in the distance
last night two curious

foxes   young ones
came by for the wild
salmon cooking on
the gas grill

can one be stead
fast now   see
clearly & with
joy at dawn

      a male & female
      cardinal at the bird
      feeder & the red
      azaleas blooming along

            the fence line
            all this before
            you check the daily
            death count

i am ready
to become something
else   am i
really   dissolve

dissolute   to face
or turn away from
who said *or* ?
this is it

& when the virus
hit   can we
change   or does
connection break away

the treasure store
is open you
can take what
you want — no

    you can take
    what you need
    through practice
    you may learn

        to receive what
        is already yours
        here is the bell sound
        to awaken you

i gave birth
to you   which means
i also gave you
death   & now

      my mother   you
      find yourself – fever
      spiking 104 – in
      an ambulance alone

         late at night
         on the way to
         the hospital to
         ICU & tests

hard to remain
calm listening to
the death toll
knowing that change

     & impermanence
have always been
our nature   but
there is that gap

       fear that takes us
far away from
what we think
we know

i think
you are
on your way
& it pains me

      that i
      that no one
      can be
      with you

            what you are
            what you were
            dissolving into the virus
            at age 89

which is a number
among many other
numbers   your fever
antibodies   the death

        count by state
        & nation & planet
        we study the numbers
        & make projections

                as the wave
                sweeps over us
                & some are
                swept away

when the Liar attacks
the students of fact
when the Liar says
everything is great

    when he is the parasite
    arrived before the virus
    when he finds enough hosts
    to sustain his disease

        when he can't find enough
        machines to keep us breathing
        when he says it every day
        with a grin and a shrug

& who
will be
the last person
with you

    & who
    will be near
    but unable
    to hold your hand

        & who
        will tell the story
        of what
        the numbers mean

what to do
in these perilous
times   he
told me

       simply
       be as you
       are
       each breath

              continues to take
              place in
              the fullness
              of time

soldier   shoulder
slow words emanate
invasion
of the invisible

      "burdens are from God
      & shoulders also"
      we are becoming
      their host

        a beautiful spring day
        in the moment   nothing changes
        in this instant   memory of the dead & dying
        to see all beings   as they are   disappearing

my door way is darkness
i trust the night time
my door way is early morning
i trust in the light

     together we walk
     the greening hillside
     young dog runs
     down   white cows amble

          across muddy pasture
          above tree line clouds
          light darkness   i sit with
          a slowly changing cedar tree

yes   i will
go up to
the stars
this language

        that we are
        goes only so far
        in peril
        of the invisible

                quiet running water
                yes
                i will go up
                to the stars

COVID19 SUTRA 2

(flattening the curve)

moving in the cloud
of unknowing   instead
i plan passover dinner
i do not know

    what is liberation
    today what would it
    mean for all of us
    to be free from

        bondage   instead of
        lamb's blood we mark our doors
        with numbers & distance
        given us by our sciences

we hurry to find
a cure we hurry
to find a vaccine
we hurry to assign

      blame   we want to
      know its gene sequence
      we want to intervene
      some cities are

            reopening   in others
            the virus has barely
            arrived   & again we
            are not equal to the task

upturned gold
& yellow
chalices of the
large oak   how

     is this possible
     then a group of
     seven deer scatters &
     then a brief skulking

          silhouette   coyote
          moving away along
          the lake trail
          up above

i will
now or
later
disappear into

     this place
     perfect
     hillside
     light shadow

        & a view
        of the pasture
        having become
        this changing light

so you say
beings of the way
cold rain to
coltrane pain becomes

    a window &
    a door way
    avalokiteshvara
    breathes in all

        suffering & ex
        hales compassion
        will we listen to this
        moment   & change

three brown dogs
at rest after
running the dew
covered hillside

      one human sits
      reading & writing
      still
      in motion

            what is happening
            remains
            far away
            & near

turn   turn
again sweet
quatrain
of the moment

    once upon a
    now & again
    host to
    our destruction

        inequality   poverty   &
        willful ignorance
        made shamefully visible
        by the disease

& what will we
do   & i don't
mean the elusive
vaccine   but really

          what will we do
          cut our hair
          go bowling a
          return to normal

                    won't do
                    as our normal
                    is precisely what
                    is failing us now

the Liar is a buffoon
let this huckster
inject bleach
into himself

the herd immunity
we need is
to *him*
we stand

exposed to
the virus yes
& to our own
incited fears

all shoulders
to the wheel
to love & rescue
what we have

      nearly lost –
      a habitable miraculous
      planet   &
      our care for

            one another   if
            this pandemic is not
            our clear call to change
            then surely all is lost

be
hold the day
which i
can

       not contain
       early morning sun
       rise over
       the pines

              what does this
              or any
              day have
              to say

awakened cosmos
& though
we are
of it

    mostly not
    awakened to
    that fact
    pickup truck

        rumbles up
        the gravel road
        incense   coffee   three dogs
        morning light

oscillating metric
of the big
picture   the death
count   the pro

      jections & the many
      unknowns
      &
      the immediate present

            moment   sudden
            beauty of its
            specific
            characteristics

here we are
&   "the whole body
is far beyond
the world's dust"[1]

      apart & together
      we gather
      by means of our
      devices

            how many are truly
            well &
            what does it mean
            to return

---

1   Dogen, *Fukanzazengi*

COVID19 SUTRA 3

(phased reopening)

who
awakens to
the bell
word music happens

      as mind
      in tribute to
      morning light
      is

            finding a way
            to be
            quiet
            again

as the virus mu
tates so too
word weird wired
would away upon

      useless play mu
      sic not beholden to
      but for its own sake
      immune to slogans &

            a manipulative daily dose
            of hope   step it up
            step it down
            clear-eyed

it is quiet
they are
at rest
am i meant

      to write
      this way
      it seems so
      what then to

            make of
            yesterday morning's
            half moon above
            the cedar tree

to de
cipher every
thing from
the virus to

      particulars of
      this instant of
      consciousness
      rest

           in the openness
           of mind   the cat
           & three dogs
           need to be fed

because everything now
occurs under the sign
of the corona virus
i wear this mask

      for you   it
      is the least
      that i can do
      same goes for gloves

          & the distance
          between us   &
          what we do
          through this poem

we are in this
to   gather
it happens quickly
fern   gardenia   crepe

      myrtle   who are
      you separate from
      this tree
      come again

          say what
          each takes a
          different path
          through disaster

all at risk
cause of death?
birth   generative
emptiness   this

    moment neither
    birth nor death
    downy woodpecker
    at the birdfeeder

        grass filling in
        bare spots
        hydrangeas soon
        to bloom[1]

---

1   This poem & the next one are dedicated to Rob Alley.

are you conscious
now   think it
as you read
these words   then

      there is a
      gap   &
      you are some
      where else

            do you see
            the red-breasted
            grosbeak   are you
            conscious now

No way to be sure this is really it.
What did you do to achieve it?
I did nothing – nothing at all.
Somehow you already knew what it was.

It happened while I was sitting still.
It must have had something to do with morning
    light.
Crows came to the bird feeder & found it empty.
Squirrels moved slower than usual, & the cat was
    asleep.

If it hadn't been for you, though you are miles
    away …
Sentences make you think something is certain.
How long has it been since you had a complete
    check-up?
Eventually, they say, we will all get it.

how will you
know it   &
how do you
know if you

      have it you
      probably do
      have it
      but show

            no signs
            everyone is
            capable of
            getting it

dappled light on pine
bark   i am
what i see
otherwise

     i am
     not   who
     do you
     know who

         knows what it
         is   topsoil
         to fill in
         bare spots

white-breasted nuthatch
not sure i've
ever seen the red-breasted
nuthatch   male bluebird

     goes back & forth
     from bird house nest
     to sit atop rusted
     trellis   how does

          the disease jump
          from one animal –
          a bird   a rat –
          to us   watch out

There is something underneath it all.
A temple in the ear, a temple in the heart, a
    temple in the mind.
The music played is never the same twice.
I am here now & see only a small fraction of it.

The pictures of Jupiter answer some of the
    questions.
This world here & your life in time are not what
    you think they are.
If it is a cloud of unknowing know that the cloud
    like any weather is constantly changing.
I asked what she had been reading & she gave
    me quite a list.

How & why some come to know it & others do
    not.
For a brief time – a life time – consciousness
    alights on a body like a butterfly drawn to a
    bright flower.
I can't get rid of the middle-aged woman in
    Jarrell's poem shouting "you know what I was,
    you see what I am, change me, change me!"
Written under the sign of the virus, written under
    the sign of the present moment.

am i   are you
conscious now
snap to   remember
to wear the mask

                in public   compassion &
                peace emanate from you
                alive in the primal word-hoard
                treasure of incremental

                        knowing   we make
                        adjustments   tinker
                        with our posture
                        over hours of sitting

COVID19 SUTRA 4

(we're back?)

actuality is not
flat   this morning
the voice has not
entered me   shadowy

      light through pines
      to see it steadily
      peace & compassion
      are these the voice

            it itself remains
            the question   head
            heart hand   trans
            mission is happening

we could think
about it forever
walking upon the bare
ground   i look down

    transparent   eyeball
    i have no head
    i never did
    it all passes

        through me i am
        a door way   a portal
        an occasion by which
        it arrives

magical catalyst
read this   remember
something else   mind
in tranquility sees

       it as it
       arises it is
       place that shelters
       you   know one

              place well   changing
              light   seasonal
              dance of green & gold
              this happens to you[1]

1   This and the following two poems are for José Kozer.

We debate the meaning of the numbers.

Infection count, death count, caught in a time
delay.

Death of logic, death of rationality, science
becomes something to believe or not.

Once that verb gets introduced, science finds
itself cast into a space where it perishes.

The future has contracted into now & the next
few months.

Pileated woodpecker pounds the railing of the
deck.

Whoever told you that observing your mind was
easy?

I can't live like this all the time.

We already are self-driving cars.

Nothing so pleasing as that first bowel movement
of the day.

Hydrangeas are beginning to bloom & a few
gardenias too.

Time & change: listen to the tune underneath it
all.

meaning cannot be
extracted from daily
reality so don't
expect it in a

      poem   cascade
      of overlapping bird
      calls traffic & human
      activity mix with

            wind through trees
            who would seize
            on one thing
            over another

The visitor insinuates himself among us.

He is not from here not from now, he is not
familiar with our ways.

Cast a cold eye on life, cast a cold eye on death,
horseman fly by.

It is not exactly how you remember it.

The visitor cannot understand what we do to
one another; he cannot understand why we
make such a big deal about our different
appearances.

Who can name the trees & birds in your own
backyard.

She is very afraid, but she still has a job (&
benefits).

We call them "heroes" & "essential" but we will
not pay them a living wage nor will we keep
them safe.

The orange-faced Liar with raccoon eyes says,
"vaccine or no vaccine, we're back."

Put your thumbs up & honk your horns.

Bar graphs & pie charts served daily.

Just how much can you stand to know?

we remain a
question to
ourselves
questionable

      enigma beings
      determined
      to know
      what being

            is   & then
            there is this to
            deal with   which
            is too much to think about

is &
it
gnats
among bigger words

    my life or
    yours
    one among many
    destined

        to be for
        gotten
        what is *that*
        tapping at the door

it is
his odd
cadence that i
remember

        carry forward
        or my father's
        posture
        hand on hip

            return to
            the breath
            which is
            everyone's

Beyond the door was much the same.

They had quarantined, they had sheltered in
place, & now the door stood open by order of
the Liar.

Because it is invisible, because it depends upon
the telling of science, many pretended it didn't
exist.

Hydrangeas bloom, gardenias too, spring turned
humid with afternoon thunderstorms.

Some asked, "who am I," and "what really
matters."

Some learned quickly to love the quiet isolation.

Some couldn't stand it, & they beat their wives &
children.

The Liar kept naming others to blame for it all.

Predictions varied about what will happen in the
fall.

Some got it right, some didn't, some said money
& greed would determine the plan.

A million died with no family & no friends at
their bedside.

Each community & each state handled it
differently: let a million deaths bloom.

an interwoven
tissue   cosmos
existing & pushing
us toward mutual

      awareness   through
      me & you writing
      poems about itself
      joy of such moments

            arising & dissolving
            i love this world
            more
            than i had thought

It will never be over; it will never go away.

Red-bellied woodpecker & white-breasted nuthatch cling differently to bark of the pine tree.

It is a test of our cleverness; it is a test of our compassion.

The bloom-color depends upon acidity of the soil.

Like grapes, tomatoes have an exactness of taste specific to variety & location.

I retreated from big cities nearly fifty years ago.

Melville's The Confidence Man (published on April Fool's Day 1857) foretold it all: the huckster, the salesman, the liar at the heart of American life.

By means of this technology at hand as a group we sit together in silence.

What is there to see, what is there to say, now extends its way throughout the universe.

We can't see them but there are plenty of other worlds happening right now.

I am glad that every now & then we can have this conversation.

I still cannot tell you what consciousness is.

there's nothing there
when are you
when called into
being

aware of it
before it all
gets organized
into the already

known   cat
at the back door
wants in
you know what to do

"We inherited a broken, terrible system," Trump told
    reporters on April 18. "Our cupboards were bare. We
    had very little stockpile."[1]
Branches of the gardenia bush bow down overflowing
    with blossoms.
"Trump can lie, but the numbers cannot. Obama
    left office with an unblemished record of building
    up the nation's pandemic preparedness. Trump
    systematically sought to dismantle it."
The new sod – centipede – is beginning to take root
    filling in the bare patches.

"By Obama's final year, the nation's preparedness on
    all measurements was 98% to 100%. That's by the
    Trump administration's own assessment."
If it's not possible to sit in the morning, I sit in the
    afternoon.
"If the cupboard was bare, it's because Trump swept it
    clean."
Typically drawn in the shape of a quickly & expertly
    drawn not fully closed zero, the *ensō* itself displays a
    generative emptiness.

"Vaccine or no vaccine, we're back," says Trump. (May
    15, 2020)
"He was just in a fucking rage. He was saying, 'This is
    so unfair to me! Everything was going great. We were
    cruising to re-election!'"[2]
"American virus deaths at 100,000: What does a
    number mean?"[3]
"We're back." ? My ass, you stupid motherfucker. As if
    a cloud came over me…

---

1   The initial four quotationas are from *St. Louis Post-Dispatch*, May
    25, 2020.

2   Gabriel Sherman, *Vanity Fair*, May 26, 2020.

3   Associated Press headline, May 27, 2020.

COVID19 SUTRA 5

("I can't breathe")

oh lord the light
i am
as you are
gone over to

    what is
    happening now
    no way to
    be outside

        this invisible
        & perilous
        presence   oh lord
        the morning light[1]

---

1   This and the following poem are for Rick Fitzgerald.

just
as it is
to see
clearly

      means to know
      one bird from
      another   house finch
      (carpodacus mexicanus)   from

            purple finch   downy from
            hairy woodpecker   as
            in all things   to
            look closely   & slowly

one   & then
the other
who is it
beneath

    that mask
    take joy for
    instance
    how long

        does it last
        esther phillips sings
        "don't put no
        headstone on my grave"

early morning high up
a pine tree one
then two then
a smaller third

      as i had hoped
      three or four weeks
      ago from the calls
      i heard in the nearby woods

          indeed a family
          of pileated woodpeckers &
          i am gone
          in the watching

they are en
trusted to us
& that is
how we know

the years
all this immediacy
joy & pain
while the Liar

inflicts his damage
that is how
we know
the days

We imagine what it will be like afterwards.

Each has a dream, each has a life, & there is also
the middle way.

I've been doing this for fifty years, but what he
wrote me about the simplest poem made me
weep for joy.

She is old; it is unclear to me what she is barking
at.

Writing the facts & figuring out their best
sequence turns out to be the hardest of all.

In a month, when I turn 70, I may, after 55 years,
take a vow to return to playing the piano.

You cannot force a child to love something.

The Liar said, "when the looting starts, the
shooting starts," said it with an ominous smile
on the orange & white face of his.

Of course he won't wear a mask: it would be
redundant.

The gray cat asleep in the chair is equal to or
greater than the Liar.

It must drive him crazy that nothing's own doing,
nothing doing, *wu-wei,* is much stronger than
he could ever be.

And what would you say, like Avalokiteshvara
– all hands & eyes, to this morning light,
dew bestowed on weeds & wildflowers, ever
changing revelation of the hillside.

tools to see
how you are
doing at any
given point

     i recall two
     points determine
     a line   we have
     graphs to study

          immediacy is
          another thing
          i study light
          on the hillside

three brown dogs
run the hill
side tails quivering
noses to the

      ground   i
      amble behind
      them in my
      own slow

         way of knowing
         this moment
         which of course
         includes the invisible

Police are protecting the governmental structures
   which the demonstrators wish to burn down.
A sentence makes a declaration, of
   independence, of confinement, or death, but
   once it gets started it must say something.
If you are thinking "what pandemic, what
   virus?" simply because you are eating a plate
   of sautéed garbanzo beans, rainbow chard,
   shaved parmesan, cilantro, & fresh linguine,
   & a crisp white wine, in this moment you are
   very right and very wrong.
Too many qualifiers, too many if's and but's: let's
   cut to the chase.

Or, as my great uncle Leon, a great arguer
   himself, used to say: give me a one-armed
   lawyer.
I picture José up at dawn in his small apartment
   near Miami writing the most amazing poems
   while his beloved Guadalupe prepares
   breakfast.
It seems my 89-year-old mother is always making
   cheese toast & coffee & taking pills no matter
   when we call her.
All my sister, all anyone, wants is to be listened
   to, for you to ask her what she is doing.

Each sentence is a short story: the Liar plays to
his base.
After running the dew-covered hillside, three
wet brown dogs sleep on the bare wooden floor
while I try to write a few essential sentences.
He is a dear friend & a wise one for reminding us
that your happiness is your own responsibility.
I think with love of two poets & their cat
Whitman holed up in a small apartment in
Oakland.

away in a
manger or
way up in
space it

all happens at
once holding
in mind   *todos*
los seres

en todos los
mundos   all suffering
become
a transcendental blues

each day is
rich
in its
specifics

    an interruption
    is not
    an interruption
    it is

        the content of
        the day   the bell
        sounds concluding
        our meditation

only recently discovered[1]
i have a
brother
age eighty

    traveling
    the Way
    hidden in
    a small apartment

        near Miami
        writing each morning
        viviendo y escribiendo
        la verdad de la casa

---

1   for José Kozer, *por supuesto*

Yes, shattered glass, burning buildings, these are
the voices of the unheard, mixed in with others
intent on something else.
In the 1960s, they had infiltrated every group I
was a part of; where is the FBI now?
The orange-faced Liar stays in his bunker;
around midnight his anger bubbles over & he
hammers out a string of incendiary tweets.
Who calls for calm must be a practitioner of same.

After sitting, then again wake to the world &
go out into it, some masked, many not, each
imagining & living in a different reality,
perhaps as it had been well before this
happened.
The Liar makes it simple: keep the economy
going, protect buildings & businesses, attack
those who disagree.
If you do not take care of yourself, what else can
you do.
A sentence still contains within it a poem.

Laughter happens, as it should.
Who was the man who died, & who was his
killer?
Ask the ones with eyes & hands, ask the one
whose heart is breaking, ask the one who hears
their cries.
Rest in the openness of mind.

so that the words
equality justice democracy
mark something other
than our shame

      pain goes straight
      to our emptiness
      repeated videos enshrine
      the victims   what to do

         with two viruses
         death of a nation
         blurred as i age
         into what's next

Hank Lazer has published thirty-two books of poetry, including *Slowly Becoming Awake (N32)* (2019, Dos Madres Press), *Poems That Look Just Like Poems* (2019, PURH – one volume in English, one in French), *Evidence of Being Here: Beginning in Havana (N27)*, (2018, Negative Capability Press), and *Thinking in Jewish (N20)* (2017, Lavender Ink). Previous books include *Poems Hidden in Plain View* (2016, in English and in French), *Brush Mind: At Hand* (2016). Lazer has performed jazz-poetry improvisations in the US and Cuba with musicians Davey Williams, Omar Pérez, Andrew Raffo Dewar, Holland Hopson, and others. In 2015, Lazer received Alabama's most prestigious literary prize, the Harper Lee Award, for lifetime achievement in literature. Lazer has been quarantining in Tuscaloosa, Alabama, and at Duncan Farm in Carrollton, Alabama.

Praise for *COVID19 SUTRAS*

Hank Lazer precisely notates the passing of time through pandemic and uprising. Consciousness alights on each poem "like a butterfly drawn to a bright flower," offering luminous company in dark times.

—Charles Bernstein, poet, author of *The Pitch of Poetry*

I imagine I join many who are celebrating with you this deeply meaningful culmination and contribution. I like to think it's you joining the demonstrations—a poet in the time of two virusesbecoming a lived answer to your question what to do. When the future seems "contracted into now and the next few months" I was grateful to join you on a sutra-linking journey for finding one's way forward into greater openness and hope.

—Dr. Linda Goodman, psychoanalyst

Simply put I found these words are a requiem for the living and dead. Poetry masterfully choreographed that speaks to our past, present and future selves. I loved this work.

—Cornelius Carter, choreographer, and a US Case Carnegie Professor of the Year

In this gorgeously powerful book, Hank Lazer, one of our great poets, turns his attention to the Covid 19 pandemic. Lazer's brilliant language opens and deepens; his awareness gives us strength; his poems' layers and pathways arrange the essential, and horrifying, facts, thereby enacting and embodying emotion and thought, teaching us to feel and think in and through the impossible. Lazer writes: "yes I will / go up to / the stars / this language // that we are / goes only so far / in peril / of the invisible // quiet running water / yes / I will go up / to the stars" and "so that the words / equality justice democracy / mark something other / than our shame // pain goes straight / to our emptiness." *COVID19 SUTRAS* is profound and magical, and to say that these poems are wise and humane is a radical understatement, like saying that water is helpful to life.

—Joseph Lease, poet, author of *The Body Ghost*

Hank Lazer's poetry has always traced the ways we navigate time. In *COVID19 SUTRAS*, he writes into and through this time of crises in poems alternatively meditative and wild with grief. He takes a census of backyard birds before checking the death count. I'm grateful for the way he documents this complicated and perilous moment.

—Rae Armantrout, poet, author of *Wobble* and *Conjure*

"It is difficult / to get the news from poems / yet men die miserably every day / for lack / of what is found there," wrote William Carlos Williams. Hank Lazer's new book, published in the middle of a pandemic, brings us the news in the way that 18th century ballad broadsides did to Londoners. Quatrain by quatrain, Lazer sings the present world, its viruses (covid and structural racism), and its beauties (animals, friendship, the shape of a sentence). Navigating a path between journalism and sacred text (the sutra), Lazer reaches for a middle way—call it survival—in this difficult time.

—Susan M. Schultz, poet, author of *I Want to Write an Honest Sentence*

In *COVID19 SUTRAS*, Lazer's thread of close attention (i.e., love) companions us along the razor's edge. As we "check the daily/death count" and wonder "who/ will be/the last person/with [us]," Lazer stops to see the gifts of our lives reflected in forms from "cold rain to/coltrane," and a "greening hillside" where a "young dog runs." He reminds us that, if we can let it, "pain becomes a window" and that in this time of "finding a way/to be/quiet/again," we might "return to/the breath/ which is everyone's."

—Gillian Parrish, poet, author of *supermoon* and *of rain and nettles wove*

"There is something underneath it all." As the world surrendered to panic and despair Hank Lazer sat, listened and recognized something more substantial beneath the noise. The COVID-19 virus has brought him to a new place in his poetry that is experimentally spontaneous while remaining true to the Buddhist aesthetic of seeing things as they are and rendering that reality in words. Though words may ordinarily distance us, these poems make the world immediately available. What we have in these sutras is the moment of creation, the opening through which everything emerges. From that moment we receive hope and consolation: "my door way is darkness/ i trust the night time/ my door way is early morning/ i trust in the light". There is a clarity here that sustains us despite the daily onslaught of information and hype. Lazer does not seek to escape it, he notices that he too is caught in that tide, but he sees through all of it a deeper demand, a "call to change," and perhaps some sense of resolution. First and last, he remains a poet working at human being, who remembers that whatever may come we must "rest/ in the openness/ of mind."

—**Jake Berry**, poet, musician, artist, and author of *Brambu Drezi*

A distant and yet direct echo of the alarm gong first sounded by Thoreau, Lazer's poems trace an unmistakable tree ring in our shared memory, a record of our collective experience with the COVID-19 as a disastrous fallout of the industrial haste and waste forewarned by the New England sage many reincarnations ago. Ironically, in these quiet quatrains, we feel the urgency to hurry, to stop the cycle of destruction, and to cleanse the world of lies and the Liar. In Lazer, we find a poetic soul patient as a rice counter, vigilant as a firefighter, and visionary as a prophet.

—**Yunte Huang**, author of *Charlie Chan*

When Hank Lazer writes in his new *COVID19 SUTRAS*, "my door way is darkness/ i trust the night time/ my door way is early morning/ i trust in the light" [in delight] or "be/ hold the day/ which i/ can/ not contain" I immediately feel that poetry exists. And it exists in its manifold variations as a work forever in progress, beyond ourselves, shifting and moving along whether as visual or linear writing, in its ability to sustain a reader's interest and to me interest in devotion.

—**José Kozer,** poet, author of *Of Such A Nature / Índole*, a Montgomery Fellow, and recipient of the Pablo Neruda Prize for Poetry

In *COVID19 SUTRAS* Hank Lazer resumes his ongoing project of thinking as/with/through/in the poem. These lucid quiet short lyrics live *in peril/of the invisible*, against a background of birds, dogs, and pastoral landscapes. *My doorway is darkness/I trust in the night/my doorway is early morning/I trust in the light.* To engage fully with the world as it is now, beyond the destabilizing clatter of the daily news cycle, we need what these poems offer: sanity, and deep care. *I love this world/more/than I had thought.*

—Norman Fischer, Zen priest, poet, author of author of *on a train at night* and *untitled series: life as it is*

The treasury of days chronicled here in sutra, like Avalokiteshvara in prayer, represent canonical hours of keeping the faith, daily observations in the fullness of quarantined time. It continues Lazer's ongoing meditations on developments in the natural world in response to the infected body politic. This is a true account of economy, devotion, and the stations of incremental knowing that take root in the evening and the morning light, transmission and proximity, environment and humanity, care of animals and the soul, and all the phenomena between them.

—Glenn Mott, poet, author of *Eclogues in a Mustard Seed Garden*

"The world is too much with us; late and soon…" Wordsworth invented the Romantic ache but we inhabit the whole howl now. The prescient poems of Hank Lazer's instant classic, *COVID19 SUTRAS*, kept re-minding me that the alphabet of our DNA is a mere four letter seismic syncopation and that a virus unzips and re-sutures the protein strands of life with atonal improvisations of our demise. These sutras steep us in the sentiment of loss and the sentimental power of belonging to longing. Though slight, these mere slips of the tongue tease these lines. They too are too much with us. They stick. They sting. They singe. They sing. They machine, in their elegance and élan, the out of tune harmonic of this time and this place. Each is a tap and die tool set that creates a threaded telling string theory for our unraveled and unraveling world.

—**Michael Martone** author of *Brooding* and *The Moon Over Wapakoneta*

Lavender Ink
New Orleans

Made in the USA
Middletown, DE
07 August 2020